Thrive!

AN APPLICATION JOURNAL TO DISCOVER YOUR STRENTGH

This Journal Belongs to:

_____

Thrive!
An Application Journal to Discover Your Strength
Copyright © by April H. Collins

Requests for information can be emailed to:

author@onlythestrongthrive.com

Scriptures taken from the ESV® Bible (the Holy Bible, English Standard Version®), copyright © 2001 by Crossway, a publishing ministry of Good News Publishers. Used by permission. All rights reserved. Scriptures taken from the New King James Version®, copyright © 1982 by Thomas Nelson. Used by permission. All rights reserved. Scriptures taken from the Holy Bible, New International Version®, NIV®, copyright © 1973, 1978, 1984, 2011 by Biblica, Inc.™ Used by permission of Zondervan. All rights reserved.

ISBN: 978-1-7325473-3-9

All rights reserved. No part of this journal may be reproduced or transmitted in any form or by any means, electronic or mechanical, including photocopying and recording, or by any information storage or retrieval system, without permission in writing from the publisher.

Published in the United States by April H. Collins.

Printed in the United States

onlythestrongthrive.com
facebook.com/authoraprilhcollins
twitter.com/author_acollins

Custom Chapter Title Artwork by: Teale Yeilding | Lettering + Design

Thrive!

This Application Journal should be used in conjunction with the book, ***Only the Strong Thrive: A True Story of Struggle, Perseverance, and Triumph***. In the book, I share my life experiences and some of the challenges I overcame to finally learn to live a fulfilled life. I developed the journal because I wanted readers to have a place to process the book's concepts in an organized and meaningful way.

While developing this journal, I envisioned small groups of women and girls gathering together to share their individual stories after exploring each chapter in the book. While the journal will be helpful for individuals, it is also perfect for small groups, Bible study groups, and book clubs. My hope is that this journal will help facilitate conversations at kitchen tables, in living rooms, coffee shops, office break rooms, and in other settings across the world!

Each section of the journal has five parts: Meditate, Prompt, Affirm, Reflect, and Note. First, *Meditate* on the Bible verse and thoughtfully respond to each *Prompt*. Next, *Affirm* the strength you possess by writing and reciting the statements in each section. Then, *Reflect* on the content you connected with while reading the book. Finally, *Note* your feelings in free and expressive writing.

The strength to overcome life's challenges is already within you. Together, this application journal and ***Only the Strong Thrive*** will encourage you to use your strength to build the future you desire. I pray you are immensely blessed by both the book, ***Only the Strong Thrive,*** and ***Thrive!*** An Application Journal to Discover Your Strength.

- April H. Collins

1
To Thrive or to Survive?

Meditate.
-Feed Your Heart-

"I am come that they might have life, and that they might have it more abundantly."
John 10:10

Date_____

1. Define "abundant life". In what ways do you feel you can live your life more abundantly?

_____
_____
_____
_____
_____
_____
_____
_____
_____
_____
_____
_____
_____
_____

And He said to me, "My grace is sufficient for you, for My strength is made perfect in weakness." 2 Corinthians 12:9 NKJV

2. Describe a time when you questioned your ability to overcome a challenge. How were you able to overcome your challenge?

_____
_____
_____
_____
_____
_____
_____
_____
_____
_____
_____
_____
_____
_____

3. Have any outside influences discouraged you from pursuing a goal in life? What is the best way to drown out the negativity?

_____
_____
_____
_____
_____
_____
_____
_____
_____
_____
_____
_____
_____
_____

And He said to me, "My grace is sufficient for you, for My strength is made perfect in weakness." 2 Corinthians 12:9 NKJV

1. I can live an abundant life because of the life Jesus Christ lived.

_____
_____

2. I have strength, through Jesus Christ, to overcome any challenge.

_____
_____

3. No one and nothing will prevent me from living the life I was designed to live.

_____
_____

Reflect on any part(s) of the chapter in the book that resonated with you. How can you apply any lessons learned to your life?

_____
_____
_____
_____
_____
_____
_____
_____
_____
_____

And He said to me, "My grace is sufficient for you, for My strength is made perfect in weakness." 2 Corinthians 12:9 NKJV

NOTE.
-Free Writing-

2
Strength in Adversity

"We are afflicted in every way, but not crushed; perplexed, but not driven to despair; persecuted, but not forsaken; struck down, but not destroyed."
2 Corinthians 4:8-9

Date_____

1. Identify a negative circumstance that occurred in your life. Write and discuss how you can use that circumstance as a source of strength.

_____
_____
_____
_____
_____
_____
_____
_____
_____
_____
_____
_____
_____

And He said to me, "My grace is sufficient for you, for My strength is made perfect in weakness." 2 Corinthians 12:9 NKJV

2. Describe a moment you felt bitterness or resentment about your circumstances. Did your feelings bring about a positive result?

_____
_____
_____
_____
_____
_____
_____
_____
_____
_____
_____
_____
_____
_____

3. What lessons have you learned as a result of adversity?

_____

_____

_____

_____

_____

_____

_____

_____

_____

_____

_____

_____

_____

_____

_____

_____

_____

_____

_____

_____

And He said to me, "My grace is sufficient for you, for My strength is made perfect in weakness." 2 Corinthians 12:9 NKJV

1. I am strong in spite of my circumstances.

_____
_____

2. I can turn a negative situation into a positive result.

_____
_____

3. My circumstances will not hold me back.

_____
_____

Reflect on any part(s) of the chapter in the book that resonated with you. How can you apply any lessons learned to your life?

_____
_____
_____
_____
_____
_____
_____
_____
_____

And He said to me, "My grace is sufficient for you, for My strength is made perfect in weakness." 2 Corinthians 12:9 NKJV

NOTE.
-Free Writing-

3
The Strength to Conquer Fear

"For God hath not given us the spirit of fear; but of power, and of love, and of a sound mind."
2 Timothy 1:7

Date_____

1. Has fear prevented you from taking a desired action? How can/did you conquer it?

_____
_____
_____
_____
_____
_____
_____
_____
_____
_____
_____
_____
_____
_____

And He said to me, "My grace is sufficient for you, for My strength is made perfect in weakness." 2 Corinthians 12:9 NKJV

2. What goal would you set if you <u>KNEW</u> you would succeed?

_____
_____
_____
_____
_____
_____
_____
_____
_____
_____
_____
_____
_____
_____
_____

3. Using the 4-step process described in the book, what specific steps can you take to conquer a current fear?

___

And He said to me, "My grace is sufficient for you, for My strength is made perfect in weakness." 2 Corinthians 12:9 NKJV

1. I have the strength to conquer fear.
   _____
   _____

2. God is with me, and with Him all things are possible.
   _____
   _____

3. I have the power to WIN!
   _____
   _____

Reflect on any part(s) of the chapter in the book that resonated with you. How can you apply any lessons learned to your life?

_____
_____
_____
_____
_____
_____
_____
_____
_____
_____

And He said to me, "My grace is sufficient for you, for My strength is made perfect in weakness." 2 Corinthians 12:9 NKJV

NOTE.
-Free Writing-

4
Strong Faith

Meditate.
-Feed Your Heart-

"He replied, 'Because you have so little faith. Truly I tell you, if you have faith as small as a mustard seed, you can say to this mountain, 'Move from here to there,' and it will move. Nothing will be impossible for you.'"

Matthew 17:20

Date_____

1. What is the biggest faith move you've ever made? How did God respond to your move?

_____
_____
_____
_____
_____
_____
_____
_____
_____
_____
_____
_____
_____
_____
_____
_____

2. What faith move are you being asked to make at this moment? What are your reservations?

___

And He said to me, "My grace is sufficient for you, for My strength is made perfect in weakness." 2 Corinthians 12:9 NKJV

3. Recall and write about a time when God did not answer your prayer the way you would have liked. Do you trust that His will is best?

_____
_____
_____
_____
_____
_____
_____
_____
_____
_____
_____
_____
_____
_____
_____

AFFIRM.
-Write and Recite-

1. I can trust God to handle every situation in my life.

_____

_____

2. I accept God's will for my life.

_____

_____

3. My faith makes me strong!

_____

_____

And He said to me, "My grace is sufficient for you, for My strength is made perfect in weakness." 2 Corinthians 12:9 NKJV

Write your personal faith prayer. Tell God how confident you are that He will work out a specific situation in your life.

_____
_____
_____
_____
_____
_____
_____
_____
_____
_____

NOTE.
-Free Writing-

And He said to me, "My grace is sufficient for you, for My strength is made perfect in weakness." 2 Corinthians 12:9 NKJV

5
The Strength to Focus

"Let your eyes look straight ahead; fix your gaze directly before you. Give careful thought to the paths for your feet and be steadfast in all your ways."
Proverbs 4:25-26

Date_____

1. On what desired goal can you keep a laser focus? Explain how you can best keep your focus in line.

_____
_____
_____
_____
_____
_____
_____
_____
_____
_____
_____
_____
_____
_____
_____

And He said to me, "My grace is sufficient for you, for My strength is made perfect in weakness." 2 Corinthians 12:9 NKJV

2. Identify a distraction that has kept you from your desired goal. What boundaries can/have you set?

_____
_____
_____
_____
_____
_____
_____
_____
_____
_____
_____
_____
_____
_____
_____

3. What will help you get back on track when you realize you have lost your focus?

_____
_____
_____
_____
_____
_____
_____
_____
_____
_____
_____
_____
_____
_____
_____
_____
_____
_____
_____

And He said to me, "My grace is sufficient for you, for My strength is made perfect in weakness." 2 Corinthians 12:9 NKJV

1. I have the strength to focus on my desired goal.

   _____
   _____

2. Distractions will not take me off course.

   _____
   _____

3. God will give me the clarity I need in my life if I ask for it.

   _____
   _____

Reflect on any part(s) of the chapter in the book that resonated with you. How can you apply any lessons learned to your life?

_____
_____
_____
_____
_____
_____
_____
_____
_____
_____

And He said to me, "My grace is sufficient for you, for My strength is made perfect in weakness." 2 Corinthians 12:9 NKJV

NOTE.
-Free Writing-

6
The Strength to Forgive and Be Free

"Bear with each other and forgive one another if any of you has a grievance against someone. Forgive as the Lord forgave you."
Colossians 3:13

Date_____

1. Write about a time when someone hurt you. How did it affect your life?

_____

And He said to me, "My grace is sufficient for you, for My strength is made perfect in weakness." 2 Corinthians 12:9 NKJV

2. Have you forgiven the person who hurt you? If not, what do you need to move past the hurt and pain?

_____
_____
_____
_____
_____
_____
_____
_____
_____
_____
_____
_____
_____
_____

3. Think back to an instance when you needed to request forgiveness. Did you handle the situation the best way? If not, what can you do to make it right?

_____
_____
_____
_____
_____
_____
_____
_____
_____
_____
_____
_____
_____
_____
_____
_____

And He said to me, "My grace is sufficient for you, for My strength is made perfect in weakness." 2 Corinthians 12:9 NKJV

1. The chains of unforgiveness will not bind me.

_____
_____

2. I can forgive because God has forgiven me.

_____
_____

3. I have the strength to forgive and be free!

_____
_____

Conversations can help begin the process of forgiveness. How would you start a conversation that needs to take place? Begin it here.

_____
_____
_____
_____
_____
_____
_____
_____
_____

And He said to me, "My grace is sufficient for you, for My strength is made perfect in weakness." 2 Corinthians 12:9 NKJV

NOTE.
-Free Writing-

7
The Strength to Love

Meditate.
-Feed Your Heart-

"Love bears all things, believes all things, hopes all things, endures all things."
I Corinthians 13:7

Date_____

1. Define "love".

_____
_____
_____
_____
_____
_____
_____
_____
_____
_____
_____
_____
_____
_____
_____
_____
_____

And He said to me, "My grace is sufficient for you, for My strength is made perfect in weakness." 2 Corinthians 12:9 NKJV

2. What act(s) of love do you remember most vividly from your childhood? How do those actions impact your life today?

_____
_____
_____
_____
_____
_____
_____
_____
_____
_____
_____
_____
_____
_____

3. Have you ever allowed your feelings or selfish desires to get in the way of love? Explain.

_____
_____
_____
_____
_____
_____
_____
_____
_____
_____
_____
_____
_____
_____
_____
_____
_____
_____

And He said to me, "My grace is sufficient for you, for My strength is made perfect in weakness." 2 Corinthians 12:9 NKJV

1. I am worthy of love.

   _____

   _____

2. God's love for me does not change...ever.

   _____

   _____

3. God's love will mend my brokenness and heal all wounds.

   _____

   _____

Reflect on any part(s) of the chapter in the book that resonated with you. How can you apply any lessons learned to your life?

_____
_____
_____
_____
_____
_____
_____
_____
_____

And He said to me, "My grace is sufficient for you, for My strength is made perfect in weakness." 2 Corinthians 12:9 NKJV

NOTE.
-Free Writing-

8 Strength in Community

"Two are better than one, because they have a good reward for their toil. For if they fall, one will lift up his fellow. But woe to him who is alone when he falls and has not another to lift him up! Again, if two lie together, they keep warm, but how can one keep warm alone? And though a man might prevail against one who is alone, two will withstand him—a threefold cord is not quickly broken."

Ecclesiastes 4:9-12

Date_____

1. Describe a time someone helped you get through a challenge in life. Have you shared with them how they have impacted your life?

_____
_____
_____
_____
_____
_____
_____
_____
_____
_____
_____
_____

And He said to me, "My grace is sufficient for you, for My strength is made perfect in weakness." 2 Corinthians 12:9 NKJV

2. Write the names of 3-5 people who can help you accomplish a current goal. List specifically how each can help. Call one on the list this week.

3. Pay it forward. How can you help someone this week?

___

And He said to me, "My grace is sufficient for you, for My strength is made perfect in weakness." 2 Corinthians 12:9 NKJV

1. God blesses me through others.

   _____

   _____

2. I know people who will help me reach a goal. I just have to ask.

   _____

   _____

3. I have strength in community.

   _____

   _____

Reflect.
-Ponder and Process-

Discuss any hesitations you've had about asking for help in order to achieve a goal? What might help you get past your concerns?

_____
_____
_____
_____
_____
_____
_____
_____

And He said to me, "My grace is sufficient for you, for My strength is made perfect in weakness." 2 Corinthians 12:9 NKJV

NOTE.
-Free Writing-

9
The Strength to Move Forward

Meditate.
-Feed Your Heart-

"Not that I have already obtained this or am already perfect, but I press on to make it my own, because Christ Jesus has made me his own. Brothers, I do not consider that I have made it my own. But one thing I do: forgetting what lies behind and straining forward to what lies ahead, I press on toward the goal for the prize of the upward call of God in Christ Jesus."

Philippians 3:12-14

Date_____

1. How has your own desire for perfection led to unhealthy or unnecessary pressure in your life? Discuss ways in which you can be better and excel in those areas instead.

_____
_____
_____
_____
_____
_____
_____
_____
_____
_____
_____
_____
_____

And He said to me, "My grace is sufficient for you, for My strength is made perfect in weakness." 2 Corinthians 12:9 NKJV

2. What can you do at this moment to move forward in an area of your life?

_____
_____
_____
_____
_____
_____
_____
_____
_____
_____
_____
_____
_____
_____
_____

3. How can you strive for a more intimate relationship with God?

_____
_____
_____
_____
_____
_____
_____
_____
_____
_____
_____
_____
_____
_____
_____
_____
_____
_____

And He said to me, "My grace is sufficient for you, for My strength is made perfect in weakness." 2 Corinthians 12:9 NKJV

1. Perfection is not required of me.
   _____
   _____

2. I can live confidently in Jesus Christ.
   _____
   _____

3. I have the strength to move forward.
   _____
   _____

Reflect on any part(s) of the chapter in the book that resonated with you. How can you apply any lessons learned to your life?

_____
_____
_____
_____
_____
_____
_____
_____
_____
_____

And He said to me, "My grace is sufficient for you, for My strength is made perfect in weakness." 2 Corinthians 12:9 NKJV

NOTE.
-Free Writing-

10
The Strength to Triumph

"Now thanks be to God who always leads us in triumph in Christ, and through us spreads the fragrance of the knowledge of him everywhere."
2 Corinthians 2:14

Date_____

1. What do you think God's plan is for your life?

_____

_____

_____

_____

_____

_____

_____

_____

_____

_____

_____

_____

_____

_____

And He said to me, "My grace is sufficient for you, for My strength is made perfect in weakness." 2 Corinthians 12:9 NKJV

2. How can you use the circumstances of your life to spread the knowledge of Christ?

3. What can you do this month to place yourself in the best position to live the life God designed for you? Set a specific goal.

_____
_____
_____
_____
_____
_____
_____
_____
_____
_____
_____
_____
_____

And He said to me, "My grace is sufficient for you, for My strength is made perfect in weakness." 2 Corinthians 12:9 NKJV

1. I have the power and authority to live the abundant life God has promised.

_____
_____

2. I can make my own way in life.

_____
_____

3. I will THRIVE!

_____
_____

Think about the obstacles you have overcome in life. How can/have you turn those negative situations into positive ones? How can you use those situations to glorify God?

_____
_____
_____
_____
_____
_____
_____

And He said to me, "My grace is sufficient for you, for My strength is made perfect in weakness." 2 Corinthians 12:9 NKJV

NOTE.
-Free Writing-

And He said to me, "My grace is sufficient for you, for My strength is made perfect in weakness." 2 Corinthians 12:9 NKJV

Only the Strong Thrive: A True Story of Struggle, Perseverance, and Triumph

by April H. Collins is now available.

www.onlythestrongthrive.com

www.ingramcontent.com/pod-product-compliance
Lightning Source LLC
Chambersburg PA
CBHW071220070526
44584CB00019B/3092